FINDING YOUR WAY

after

Your Parent Dies

FINDING YOUR WAY

after

Your Parent Dies

Hope for Grieving Adults

Richard Gilbert

with a foreword by Darcie Sims

ave maria press　　Notre Dame, IN

© 1999 by Ave Maria Press, Inc.

International Standard Book Number: 0-87793-694-3

Cover and text design by Brian C. Conley

Printed and bound in the United States of America.

Library of Congress Cataloging-in-Publication Data

Gilbert, Richard B.

Finding your way after your parent dies : hope for grieving adults / Richard B. Gilbert ; with a foreword by Darcie Sims.

p.   cm.

Includes bibliographical references.

ISBN 0-87793-694-3 (pbk.)

1. Parents—Death—Religious aspects—Christianity. 2. Grief—Religious aspects—Christianity. 3. Adult children—Religious life. 4. Consolation. I. Title.

BV4906.G55 1999

248.8'66—dc21

99-23753

CIP

In memory of and dedicated to

Frederic B. Gilbert, III
Eleanor T. Gilbert
Jack Shaw
Patrick Del Zoppo
Robert Thompson
Barbara Thompson
Van F. Dittberner
Alicia Haake Dittberner
Paul Wolkovits
Frances Burns
Dr. Robert G. Toepel
John Paul Govoni
Kathryne M. Fletcher
Raymond Dausman
Lewis Nicolini
Gregory Michael Ramos
Matilda Klincewicz
Kathryn A. Jones
Carroll Anderson
John Swarmer, M.D.
R. William Neumann, M.D.
Mary Catherine Eckert Smith
Ruth Culver
Catherine E. Gourley

Contents

Acknowledgments

Each book comes with many people to thank. I thank Ave Maria Press for the invitation to write this book, and for recognizing that adults grieving their parents are often a forgotten population in need of additional help and comfort. This project has been a chance to work through some more of my own story.

My wife, Sharon, and daughter, Allison, were tireless in offering feelings, anecdotes, and stories that kept me going back to my unfinished story. Darcie Sims, colleague and cherished friend, brings all of us so much insight and inspiration as she, too, grieves for her mother and father.

Special folks continue to bless me and my ministry: The Rev. Dr. Jane Shaw, Chaplain Harold ter Blanche, the Rt. Rev. George (Tom) Smith, the Rev. Canon Vincent Strudwick, Fr. Paul Wolkovits, Dr. Jim Miller, Joy and Marv Johnson (and the Centering Corporation family), Dr. Jack Morgan, Dr. Patrick Del Zoppo, Dr. Gerry Cox, Chaplain Dale Guckenberger, Andrea Gambill (and the *Bereavement Magazine* family), Judy Richmond, Rabbi Earl Grollman, Kathy Teipen (and the National Catholic Ministry to the Bereaved family), and Sr. Mauryeen O'Brien. A special thanks to Chaplain Joe Nilsen, who continues to be a guide and friend, and who was "there for us" when he was so very needed. I am grateful, too, to the Graduate Theological Foundation for their encouragement in this project.

Finally, I thank my father and mother for being the real gift of this book, and my sister, Becky Walsh, who has validated my excursions and embellished many of the stories.

Foreword

My mother and I shared so many things: lollipops, lace hankies, hair barrettes, girlish secrets, and a passion for chocolate-covered cherries. We sang camp songs and she taught me how to make "s'mores." She showed me how to make a great meatloaf and even lump-free gravy. In fact, my mom taught me everything—except how to live without her. I was forty-three when she died, and I was devastated.

When my dad died four years later, it was another blow. He and I had shared so much: fishing, camping, hiking. We looked for elves under the fallen leaves in autumn, we made angels in the snow, and we hunted Easter eggs in the newly mowed fields. He was the best storyteller I ever heard, and I loved being the subject of many of those late-night story times. No matter how old I was, he always had a glass of water ready for me at bedtime when I visited.

My parents are gone now and so is my home. Oh, I do have a house where I live and keep my belongings, but it is not my *home*. We were a military family and moved often, and so very early I learned that "home" meant wherever my parents and I were together. But now, of course, that means nowhere at all, and I realize that I have nowhere to "be from" or to "go home to."

At the same time, it seems that my basic role in the universe has changed. I am no longer anyone's child; I must now assume the adult place at the family table and in the family portrait. How can that be? I'm not ready! There is still so much to learn, so many mistakes to make.

Our parents are the keepers of our past; they glue the pictures in our scrapbook. At the same time, they help to make our present. Even after we are grown, they are still the ones who—in one way or another—give a kiss and a bandage and somehow make it all better. Now that my parents are gone, I often find myself feeling terribly alone, terribly defenseless.

Yet there is so little understanding for a loss of this kind. Often the first thing people ask after a parent's death is how old he or she was, as if the loss of an older parent is less important. Others react to the death as if it is really nothing at all.

And so, those of us grieving a parent can find ourselves quite alone. Where do we go for warm cookies and a hug? Where is that welcoming and forgiving smile? Are we now left utterly alone, without shelter or guidance?

Dick Gilbert says no. Dick Gilbert understands my loneliness, and he has created a safe haven for the bereaved adult child. Within these pages, you will find comfort, healing, and hope. Written out of his own pain, forged from his own fire of grief, this book brings new hope to those of us who have wandered alone with our sadness and grief.

Dick has reached across his own hurt as a bereaved adult child and offered a safety net of compassion, wisdom, and practical advice to the hurting soul. With his easygoing and personal style, he offers respite as well as guidance. *Finding Your Way After Your Parent Dies* is quick to read, easy to use, and is not fluffed up with pompous theories and meaningless jargon. Dick is genuine, and every page is honest and forthright.

Even though my parents have been dead a number of years now, I find this material to be of great comfort and help. Dick invites the reader to participate, providing a "thought," an "opportunity," and a prayer at the end of each chapter. He draws his readers in and then teaches us to listen to ourselves.

You hold in your hands a valuable tool for healing for any adult who has experienced the death of a parent. For me, it is the next best thing to a hug from my dad and my mom's strawberry-rhubarb pie.

Thanks, Dick, for the hope.
May love be what you remember most.

Darcie Sims

Introduction

England was in the midst of the hottest summer of the century, or so the guides told us. The temperature was soaring well into the 90s that morning, and it was only nine o'clock. The air was oppressive and still, and everything seemed to be slowly wilting.

None of this seemed to matter, though, as I approached the entrance to Christ Church Cathedral, Oxford, for Sunday worship. I froze in my tracks, a winter chill creeping through me, leaving me shaking as others wiped their brows. There, at one of the entrances, I saw my father—greeting visitors, helping them find a seat in the cathedral. He was, as always, a classic English gentleman. And yet, at this moment, my father had been dead for five years!

I tried to move my legs. Surely there was another entrance. I turned—and there he was again, at every door, in each aisle. The fear must have been written all over me because the young priest standing with me asked me what was wrong. "It's my father," I stammered, ". . . and he's dead." The young priest, perhaps startled himself, tried to comfort me with words of scripture. It wasn't what I needed to hear.

I turned to him, now almost shouting, "But my father is dead!" He paused and then, with some apprehension, replied, "Yes, I miss my father, too." That was the connection, the remembering, I needed. Suddenly, I was able to see the significance of this moment in the context of my own experience of grief. The location was strange (although my father *had* been the head usher at our church for years), but, even there, so far from home, I was given a gift: the invitation to reconnect with my own story.

My father has been dead for seven years now, and my mother, for over two years. The episode in Oxford, and the writing about it, has reminded me that even now there are still some tears to shed, still some wonderful memories to capture and share. Even as I write these words, I realize how much I miss my mother and father.

My parents pushed me courageously into my own life and the world around me, enriching me by their love and example. Now, in their dying, I have been pushed into a new world view and new experiences as one who lives without his parents. It is no small loss. Although it is often downplayed, the death of a parent or parents can leave adult children with many kinds of sadness: a feeling of being robbed of parental safety and care; a sudden encounter with their own aging and mortality, not to mention the feeling that, in some very basic way, they are now walking life's pathway alone.

This book is offered as a gentle guide and friend to adults trying to find their way after a parent's death. It is written from my experiences as a bereavement educator and pastor/priest, but most especially as a grieving adult child. It is offered as a resource to help you claim your own sorrow, but also to reach for healing, hope, and the memories and stories that remain yours.

Some parts of the book may not be a comfortable fit for you. Maybe you have chosen another direction or moved beyond those issues in your journey. Other issues may be too close to your story and tug at you to work harder. Especially the later chapters, which address a variety of special themes, may not seem to fit. Skip around or plow through. Just be open to *your* story and needs.

I am aware that not all feelings and memories associated with a parent who has died are happy. There are challenges and difficulties when our parents are alive, and these remain after our parents have died. You may have lived in and through a troubled childhood, a divisive and conflicted family, addictions, abuse, economic hardships, or other hurts that may still feel fresh and real. I can't address every issue, but it is my hope that you will receive the nudge you need to respect your experience and get the help and healing you deserve.

Throughout this book, I will talk about the common feelings and experiences we call grief, but I will not speak in terms of "the stages of grief" because this framework can sometimes be limiting, especially when "the stages" are seen as a prescribed text or script we have to follow. There are enough people telling us what to do, how to feel, and that it is time to "move on." This book will not tell you what to do; hopefully, like a friend, it will walk with you as you find your own way.

This is a grief book and it is also a spiritual book. That is not simply because I am an Anglican priest. It is because we must recognize the connection between grief and spirituality if we are to be honest with all of our story and the profound impact grief has on us. All of us are spiritual, however we choose to claim it. All of us search for meaning, for answers, for a reason to grab hold of the tomorrows in life. That is the centerpiece we call spirituality. So it is present in this book not because of my professional status or because of the mission of my publisher. It is because grief is here and so is the need for spiritual comfort and clarity.

Each chapter concludes with a brief opportunity for reflection in the form of a "thought," an "opportunity," and a prayer. The thought will come from a variety of sources; it offers something to think about, a place to pause and reflect. You might find yourself skipping around the book just to reread these quotations. The opportunity will invite you to dig deeper into your story. (Read this book with pencil in hand!) The prayer will provide a reflection point. These are invitations to pause, to rest for a while. Take all the time you need.

So grab a pencil, reconsider your own story, and be open to new possibilities for your life.

Thought / Opportunity / Prayer

T - "We are healed of a suffering only by experiencing it to the full."

—Marcel Proust

O - Find a large piece of paper. Place the name of your deceased parent at the top. If you grieve for both parents, use two sheets. Giving yourself as much time as you need, make a list of things that come to mind that you want to remember about this person and your relationship to him or her.

P - *Caring God, you greet us on the calm plains, but also in every curve, through each detour, and in the deepest valley of trauma and fear. You are love and you understand when love has been tested, twisted, or torn from me. Walk with me. Open my eyes to see you and the healing that you bring. Help me to find my way, a way now traveled without my parent(s). Amen.*

I

First Steps on the Journey

Chapter 1

What's wrong with me?
Nothing!—You are bereaved

Do you remember Dick Louden? My guess is that it's a name forgotten. That was the character played by Bob Newhart on the "Newhart Show." What particularly struck me as funny about the character was his profession: he billed himself as the author of "how-to" books. He really believed that one could write a how-to book on any subject, and that, in every case, he was the perfect author to do it.

"How-to": in this age of instant-everything, we believe that time is money, and we will grab anything that will help us get through life with ease and haste. We have how-to books on everything from building a healthy marriage to using the Internet to making household repairs.

When it comes to grieving, though, things are different. There are no how-to books on grief. Some people may believe they can write one, and I know many bereaved who search for them, but the truth is that there is no book for *your* grief, *your* feelings, *your* readjustments to this new world without your parent(s), the many tasks that require *your* attention when your energy is at its lowest. No one knows your sorrow. No one can give meaning to your feelings, and no one dare direct or control your feelings, tell you that "you should be over this by now," or suggest (as I heard countless times), "Your Dad lived to eighty-four, and he was sick for a long time; he's better off now." Maybe he was better off, but *I wasn't!*

Wading through the advice we are given, we often grieve in silence, puzzled and occasionally fearful of our feelings. We wonder what might be "eating away at us"; we look for some ray of hope that will lead us through sorrow to life and hope. In the end, though, there is only one pathway: *your* pathway. It is the pathway of your feelings.

Even within one family, various individuals can have very different experiences of grief. Each person's journey is different, and his or her feelings give expression and meaning to those journeys. Each person—including you—must be free to move along his or her own pathway. Thomas Merton once remarked, "How do you expect to arrive at the end of your journey if you take the road to another one's city?" (James Miller, *One You Loved Has Died*, p. 8). Giving each person in your family the freedom that he or she needs will prevent these differences in grieving from becoming a source of conflict.

What follows are some suggestions, hooks on which to hang the "hats" that are part of your story.

Focus—Do what you need for yourself

Grief can bring upheaval. This is especially true when we are dealing with the death of a parent. We not only have the adjustments that are now required of us as the surviving child, but we may well have to regroup with our spouse or partner. Many families have been redefined during the dying of a parent, and now may have to find all new rituals: routines will have been crushed, the most basic daily patterns may be disrupted. And there you are in the middle of it all!

Again, it is crucial that you ask yourself what you need to do for *you*. This doesn't mean that you do things at the expense of your marriage or family, but you also cannot take care of everyone else and everything else at the expense of yourself. You may already feel you have done your share of that; now is the time to be self-focused.

What do you want for you?

- A quiet evening just to read the newspaper?
- Time to catch up on endless chores around the house?
- Control of the remote control for your favorite show?
- A good night's sleep?
- Control over your kitchen?
- Space restored in the medicine cabinet?
- A day at work without someone asking or calling?
- Jogging without feeling guilty for leaving the family?
- Someone to explain all of the hospital bills?
- Peace and quiet?

Make your own list. You don't have to justify it to others. You do have to claim it for yourself.

Feel—Let the feelings flow
- Anger
- Fear
- Guilt
- Hope
- Joy
- Despair
- Relief
- Disappointment
- Exhaustion
- Hopelessness

Do any of those sound familiar to you? Like shoes, your feelings come in a size and styles that are unique to you. Also, like shoes, your feelings are part of every step of this journey you are on.

Your feelings are what make you special. Others may judge them (there are lots of "experts" out there!) but feelings are not open to judgment, unless you allow that. Mourning, in fact, means just the opposite of controlling or condemning feelings; it means stepping aside and letting the feelings flow.

That may be tough for us. We go into our grief work with the understandings and patterns that we had before. If you have had a tendency to feel guilt and shame—especially as related to your mother or father—the death of that parent may well exaggerate those feelings, not extinguish them. Many of us are troubled with anger. My father, for example, taught me, "A proper gentleman does not get angry." It took me a long time, with the help of a therapist, to let go of that advice without feeling that it reflected poorly either on my father or on me.

Various events and challenges have occurred in the Gilbert family since my parents died: some have been times of celebration, but others have been times of great despair. In some of those difficult times, I found myself feeling that circumstances would have been less difficult if my parents were still alive. I found, in fact, that I was angry with them for dying, for abandoning me when I needed them. Then I found that I was feeling guilty for lashing out at them. I told you the feelings seldom make sense!

There are many wonderful resources available to help in dealing with your feelings. (Many of them are listed in the resource section on pp. 107-124.) Experts in the area of grief describe a large number of different patterns of dealing with feelings. There are, for example, some patterns considered more masculine and others considered more feminine. You may cry easily (pack lots of tissues in your purse or pocket!), or you might rather cheer the local football team or jog an extra mile. You may find that you fit into support groups, or you may do better talking with a friend over a beer or a cup of coffee. Some people read a lot; others prefer journaling or writing poetry. Do what works for *you*. They are *your* feelings.

Filters—Potential detours and roadblocks

All of us have internal filters. They are part of what makes us the unique people that we are. The difficulty with filters is when they take over for us and, in a sense, take from us, moving us away from our pathway to healing.

Our experience of grief will inevitably be shaped by these filters in our life. Initially, it is important simply to be aware that you have many such filters, and that they are neither good nor bad. Your culture, your gender, past experiences with loss, the nature of the relationship with your parent(s), your own health, sometimes your spirituality or religion: all these greatly influence the way you will experience the loss of your parent.

I was thinking about filters when, in the middle of writing this chapter, I watched Mark McGwire, a member of the St. Louis Cardinals baseball team, hit his sixty-second home run. With the swing of his bat, an amazing new record was set. For a moment in time, all eyes were on St. Louis. The game stopped. Cheering. Fireworks. Hugs. Jack Buck, the home announcer and himself a great veteran, was seen crying. So, too, was Mark McGwire. What was remarkable was the way in which this challenged a powerful filter that is often at work. Men frequently see themselves as needing to be strong and assume that tears are a sign of weakness. Yet, for this one moment, they were being told, "It is okay to cry."

You may want to stop to consider what kinds of filters are affecting your experience of grief. Just recognizing them gives you new possibilities, since these filters are yours to use or to set aside. You should realize that other people may not understand your decisions. Peer pressure can be very strong, and the pressure of families and ethnic groups can be even stronger. What matters is that you make choices for yourself.

Remember to be patient with yourself as you deal with the filters that affect you. They can be very deep, held in place by generations of tradition, values, and meaning. It takes time to chip away at the molding that holds them into your story. You may need specific counsel on these issues. Respect what you need.

Feed—Do healthy things

There are few things in life as demanding as grief. Put simply, it is hard work. I am reminded of the "Frank and Ernest" cartoon in which they are walking away from their car, carrying a gasoline can. One of them remarks, "I thought 'E' meant 'enough.'" All of us, too, have times when we unexpectedly brush up against "empty."

We want to sleep, but insomnia takes over. We cook big meals, but have no appetite. We tell ourselves that we really want to get to that yard work, mending, or spring cleaning, but we cannot find the energy or desire to get started. We keep grabbing a snack and wonder why the pants feel so snug. Grief is hard work, and our body can suffer because of it.

Here are some suggestions to keep in mind.
- Watch what you eat. Be sure to eat.
- Drink plenty of fluids (but not the addictive kind).
- Get some exercise.
- Do something fun.
- Remember your spiritual connections.
- Take "time-outs" from all of this.
- Watch your physical health. Respect symptoms.
- Seek help when you need it.
- If sleep is a problem (too much or too little), talk to someone about it.
- Overall, make it a priority to do what you need to do to stay healthy.

Forge—Carve out what you want for your life

Your parent's death has probably affected your life in profound ways; you may even have begun to feel that life is beyond your control. You may be saddled with a surviving parent who has many needs or demands; your marriage may need some tender care; there may be bills to pay. And, of course, there are the feelings that accompany your loss. With all of that on your plate, you may not believe you have control over your own life.

It is true that many things *are* beyond your control, but important choices about your own life are still yours. Dare to dream. Dare to hope. Dare to imagine what life can be for you. Claim rituals that heal and energize you. Take on the challenges you feel ready to accept. Forge ahead. You had no choice as to the circumstances leading to your parent's death. You *do* have the choice of grieving in healthy ways and redesigning life as you hope it will become.

*T*hought / *O*pportunity / *P*rayer

T - "Grief is a lifelong process. The pain may subside and waves of sorrow may overtake you less often, but you'll always miss the presence of that special person in your life.

"God gave you all your emotions, and each of them has a purpose in your life. In time, as your turmoil and despair lessen, you'll appreciate grief for keeping you close to your loved one in heart and memory."

—Deb Haas Abell

O - Get five 3" x 5" cards or pieces of blank paper the same size. Mark each one of them as noted below. Let them be your markers on your walk. Use the backs of them to write down notes, questions, and feelings.

F	**F**	**F**	**F**	**F**
Focus	Feel	Filter	Feed	Forge

P - *Creator God, you gave us the gift of love and the desire to share it. If love is your gift, then it is also your gift that we grieve. You know my sorrow. Travel this journey with me. Amen.*

Chapter 2

This is not like anything I've felt before.
It *is* different—Your mother or father has died

Strange things happen when we are grieving. Why did I freeze outside Christ Church Cathedral? I am sure I will never get an answer to that question. Sure, the ushers bowed with great dignity, wore French-cuffed shirts, and seemed to have the right words for every person entering the cathedral, reminding me in all these ways of my father. But that doesn't explain my unshakable feeling that I was seeing my father himself.

The "why" questions that sometimes plague us have no answers, but, after all, they are not the kind of questions that could be satisfied by information. Rather, these questions invite us (and others) into our hearts, stories, and feelings. Why did I see my father that day? I saw him because I needed to see him. I wanted him to be a part of my exciting week, my first week in my doctoral studies. I wanted him to be proud of me; I wanted him to still be my father. It wasn't craziness brought on by the excessive heat. It was about love, remembering, finding new ways to keep my father (and mother) active in my life and adventures.

Grief always involves pain and loss, but there is a special sense of loss when it is a mother or father who has died. All of a sudden, we realize that underneath it all we feel that parents are not supposed to die! Whether we are five or fifty-five, part of us wants and needs to know that our parents are always going to be there for us. The rude awakening to their mortality (and our own!) thrusts us into one of the most overlooked and neglected groups of mourners: adults dealing with the death of a parent or parents.

As one in that situation, I heard all of the most common responses from those around me. People probably meant well, but their remarks often hurt. I didn't want empty reassurances. What I really needed included:

- hugs
- safe places
- insights (when I asked for them)
- clarification (when I owned that I was wandering needlessly)
- inventive and hope-filled ways to tell and re-tell the stories that are my parents

No two deaths are alike, even for the same loss. No two adult children grieve the same way, even for the same parent. While it is somewhat true that "grief is grief," the issues that surround grieving parents are different from those of people struggling after a loved one's suicide, others whose loved one was killed by an act of violence, or young children whose brother or sister has died. In your case, a parent has died, *your* parent has died, and that is the unique piece we want to look at now.

Denial—Claim your right and need to grieve

I am generally not a violent man; I already mentioned my hesitation with expressing anger. However, if one more person said to me, "Your father lived 'til he was eighty-four; you have no right to be sad," I would not have wanted to be held accountable for my actions. "No right to be sad"? What right does anyone have to tell me how I should or should not grieve?

Yet it happens. People may mean well, but the reality is that my father and my mother have died, and I miss them. For two years after my mother's death, I avoided driving on Wall Street because that is where she died at the nursing home; I didn't want to be reminded. I had lost my parent and a shortcut home. That may sound silly, going two miles out of my way, but it was my choice and no one had the right to discredit me or my need to grieve.

While some people say things that minimize the extent or nature of grief, others simply shut down emotionally around the bereaved because they do not know what to say or what to do. It is simply very difficult, very mystifying for them when they are pulled into the sorrow of someone else.

Unfortunately, in some cases, the people around us are simply unable to fathom the depth of our sadness. The death of a parent for an adult, in particular, is a loss that is easily set aside as insignificant, routine, a death "to be expected." "Old people are supposed to die," I heard a minister say last week in his sermon. Others may remark,

"Parents are supposed to die before us. It is the right thing to do." Another myth, another hurtful remark, another person building a wall around us. Adults grieving a parent are much too often isolated and forgotten.

Even people far into adulthood can find themselves wanting to cry out to others: "My father died! My mother died! I may have to handle this alone, but I would rather sense that my loved ones, friends, members of my church, my minister or priest are willing to feed me as I reveal my hunger to them."

Of course, those grieving sometimes need small doses of "denial."

That is part of grief: a place, feeling, or attitude that says, "I think I will pause here for awhile." Sometimes we need to put our grieving "on hold" for our own well-being. It may stem from an inability or unwillingness to face some deep feelings, some scars (as we will discuss later) or some tough feelings. Or we may just be exhausted. Especially if the parent suffered a long illness, there may be a need for a period of relief from their suffering (and ours). And, of course, there are the tasks associated with arranging the funeral, unraveling the mystery we call insurance and Medicare bills, and reconfiguring a house or a family. Estates may be requiring our attention, and so can a surviving parent. So if you decide to put some things on hold for a while, you may simply be doing what is most healthy for you. Unless you are in troubled waters (which is probably *not* the case), don't let someone undermine your "denial." Listen to your heart. You'll know when it is time to move on.

Demythologizing—
Coming to terms with the way it really is

Just as we are unraveling feelings, memories, and stories, we are also unraveling the picture or relationship we have of our parents. In the midst of that sometimes unnerving process, Darcie Sims reminds us in her *TouchStones* card series, "May love be what you remember the most."

For most of us, demythologizing will be only a minor part of our grief experience; for some, however, it can be devastating. Later in this book, we will address "family secrets" and surprises. Here, we are just looking at the unraveling of feelings and things that give us different glimpses of our parents and also life without our parents.

My father was a "proper English gentleman" and a corporate executive. I so admired him, treasuring my image of a man who was extremely organized, able to keep track of every detail, a wise businessman. He died before my mother did, and it was several years later that the time came to move my mother into an assisted-living facility. Faced with the reality of closing down the house packed with fifty-three years of Gilbert memories and traditions, I volunteered to clean out my father's "business" closet.

There were all of the files, taxes, stocks and business investments, paperwork for the South Shore Band (my father was a percussionist), and decades of schedules of ushers for church and for the local civic association. My father's life story was unfolding in front of me, and, despite the deadlines for packing, I just sat on the floor with all of his papers spread around me.

I did find some information that was helpful, but mostly I was surprised by what I found: my father was good, but he wasn't the genius I expected him to be. Some of his schedules were poorly organized. Some of his financial decisions were shortsighted. Slowly I felt my father slipping off the trophy shelf. I had, at least for a time, the challenge of getting to know a different father.

It wasn't a crisis, and there were no deeply hidden secrets or scars. This experience simply serves as a reminder that oftentimes, as we move from the old to the new, some images, pictures, and stories will change, to our surprise. We will have to rethink things, reframe some images and stories, perhaps spend a little more time in some side trips we hadn't planned on. It can be unnerving, but it is part of the healing process.

Forgiveness is a word that emerges constantly in the Christian tradition. We hear over and over again how God loves us and always forgives us. Forgiveness will be a major dynamic in a subsequent chapter, but I think it also fits here. Even when our parents have not really done anything wrong, they do not live up to what *we* want them or believe them to be. Part of our healing may be to forgive them for that, to let go, to accept things as they have been, so that the old does not control or destroy us as we move toward the new.

Deployment—Moving forward, but not forgetting

"Deployment" is a word common in shipping and transportation, especially in the military. It is about moving supplies or people from one place, a base, to a war zone, disaster, or crisis that requires their presence. To "deploy" means to move forward, carefully, with a plan, making peace with the events that have moved you to where you now find yourself and yet moving you forward.

Moving forward is just that—it does not mean forgetting, "being done" with your feelings, or "finishing" your grief. The sorrow can lessen and so can the pain, but it doesn't "go away." I will never be "done" with my parents. On the "good days" I find myself less distressed about their deaths, about missing them, and I find little ways to see them still in my life.

When I wear cufflinks or use my father's pocket watch, I have a special way to connect. When I share stories with a veteran teacher, I remember the many adventures of my mother as a teacher at P.S. #5. When I travel and meet someone from Staten Island, I have another connection. When someone tells me they have been to the theater, I can remember the many Broadway shows that brought so much happiness to my parents. Not forgetting, but remembering. Not moving on or away from my memories, but moving forward to discover new ways to share the feelings and tell the story.

The death of a parent can strike some very particular and sensitive nerves, raw nerves. Some of the unique dynamics of a parent's death are captured in the quotations mentioned below. (Maybe there are others you would like to add as you work through this book.) They are all issues to consider as we begin to move ahead.

"I feel so old."

First, the death of a parent can leave us suddenly feeling somehow very old. Our parents were the "older generation," the age ahead of us, and the safety net between us and our becoming the elders of family and community. As long as they were alive, we could think of ourselves as "the youngsters," carefree and able to live in denial of our own aging and dying. Sometimes the dying process includes very tough times with medical interventions, the suffering that can accompany Alzheimer's or dementia, dealing with long-term care, and other difficult experiences. As we see this in our parents, we can begin to wonder if it foreshadows our own aging process and dying experience.

"Now I'm the one who has to be responsible."

The death of a parent can also create a tremendous sense of new responsibility. Many of us will inherit additional responsibilities when caring for a surviving parent and rebuilding our family. Some of us will take on other tasks and responsibilities because we feel obligated, either by others or ourselves. There is a hidden voice that says, "I am now the senior of the family. I must now be responsible for everyone and everything. It is what is expected of me." Does it feel that way for you?

"I feel so alone."

Losing a parent can also create a deep, and perhaps unexpected, sense of loneliness. "I have never felt so alone in my life," said one man who came to me for counseling after his father's death. Unfortunately, these feelings were misinterpreted by his wife and other family members as a critique of them. "They couldn't understand," he said, "because it wasn't about *them*, but about *me*, and about the fact that I always believed *my parents would be there for me*. Now they aren't here, and I feel so alone."

"I should have done more."

In the wake of a parent's death, we may also experience powerful feelings of guilt or shame. For most of us these feeling surface in the form of "should haves." Maybe you have found yourself thinking that you should have

- visited more often
- helped more with household chores
- cut the grass each week
- taken him/her to the doctor sooner
- not argued so much
- been a more obedient or more attentive child

This list could go on and on, and maybe you will need to take time with it. Remember that these feelings of guilt can serve simply as ways to get to the deeper issue of how much you miss your parent(s). If there is some truth in the statements, find a way to deal with it safely and therapeutically. There may be some issues that need to be examined, and you may need to work through the process of receiving forgiveness from God and from yourself. Most of us, however, simply need to stop whipping ourselves and start comforting ourselves.

"My grief is causing me to let down my partner and my family."

This is much like the quotation above, but directed to the people in your life who grieve with you. Once again, there may be some issues or truth to be explored. For most of you it is an invitation, an open door to reaffirm relationships, to mend the occasional fence, and to enjoy the time you have needed with each other, time disrupted because of issues surrounding your parents. Be forgiving of yourself; it is the pathway to letting go so that you can hold on to the memories you cherish.

"I'm scared."

Fear is another common response to the death of a parent. The overwhelming demands of grief, of restoring a family, of providing for a surviving parent, of tending to the many tasks that now require your care, can be very frightening. For many of us, our parents were the role models, the sanctuaries, the pathfinders, the people on whose laps we could climb, at least emotionally, for comfort and care. When death comes, these sources of comfort and guidance are glaring for their absence. Respect whatever fear you may feel. If you are able to recognize it and work with it, it can lead you to the next stop on your journey.

"I feel relieved."

It seemed so appropriate that my father died on All Saints' Eve. We were free to climb into the celebration and hope of the eternal truths of our faith. My father's liturgy was a grand event— brass, great singing, sharing, and, in a sense, a family "party." My father would have been pleased.

And we did have some things to celebrate. His suffering was over. It had been a long four years, his journey to death. We battled his symptoms, the tragedy of his lost memory and awareness, his times of suffering, and even sometimes the medical community. It was a time of peace, a plateau of relief.

Perhaps you have experienced something similar. Enjoy it. Share it with those around you. Don't panic, however, if you find the interlude fleeting and you start stumbling off that peak of safety. It is your way of acknowledging that now the work begins. My family certainly needed to feel relief; it was a way to understand the spiritual or eternal relief that my father now shares. It was a way of coming to terms with all that his dying was about. Then it was time for us to explore what our *living* is all about.

Other quotations may pop in and out of your thoughts. Below is some space for you to write them down. Allow them to bring meaning to your experience.

Here are some final hints for your work of deployment (and it can be hard work).

1. While you must be mindful of others in your life and close to your journey, don't forget to pay attention to yourself and what you need as you grieve.

2. While each physical action (the bank, the hospital bills, rearranging furniture, funeral arrangements) unravels feelings, let them also unravel love and hope.

3.   Don't allow the denial of others to prevent you from grieving as you need to.

4.   Troubled interpersonal dynamics that existed before your parent's death do not go away just because of a death. Sometimes they can become more difficult. Pay attention to them.

5.   Be aware of the special challenges of grieving a parent who "wasn't there" for you.

6.   You still need your surviving parent to be Mom or Dad. Don't expect him or her to replace the lost parent, and don't forget he or she is also a bereaved spouse.

7.   Remember, surprises can be gifts if you allow them to be.

8.   Don't forget your children. They are grieving, too, and often have their own wounds and needs to work through.

9.   Grief is hard work. Take care of yourself. Let your family be a gift, not just a burden.

The next step is up to you. List some "things to remember" that have become important for you. You will find that different insights are important at different points in your grieving process.

One final thought: Don't forget the traditions of your faith. Spirituality that is healthy is constantly embracing you, encouraging you, affirming you. From the Christian viewpoint we see Jesus, over and over again, reaching out with the "invitation to life." Perhaps this would be the ideal time to open yourself to Jesus in a new way, to see your sorrow as carried by Christ. Search the Psalms. Hear the inviting words of the prophets. They speak of a God who has grieved and willingly shares in our sorrow. God's affirming presence never discounts our journey or our feelings, but becomes a new presence, a new energy, so that life in its fullest may be ours again—or perhaps be ours for the first time.

Thought / Opportunity / Prayer

T - "Grief has given me a new time-frame. I measure things in now, not next week or next month. I catch as many moments as I can."

—Darcie Sims, *TouchStones*

O - Design your plan of action, day to day, moment to moment, feeling to feeling, as you do the grief work you need to do. Dare to dream; then risk to reach to make those dreams your new reality. Do something special— just for you!

P - *Dear God, some days I feel so empty, so stuck. Other days I have so much energy that I spin in a million directions and get so little accomplished. Do you understand? You are the only one who can bring a moment of clarity to my world of confusion. Amen.*

Chapter 3

I feel so shattered—my life is in pieces.
Reinvestment is hard work

- Bills stacked up everywhere.
- The lawn waiting to be cut.
- Thank-you notes: will I ever get caught up?
- Closets to empty; furniture to store.
- Decisions to be made.
- Trimming needed at the graveside.
- I need to regroup with my family.
- My spouse wants attention; I'm just too tired.
- I want attention; my spouse is too tired.
- The children have so many questions; why aren't there any answers?
- I worry about Mom/Dad staying in the house alone.
- I know my blood pressure is through the roof.
- I really miss Mom/Dad. It just isn't the same anymore.

We have talked about the common feelings and experiences we call grief. Sometimes, there is shock, fear, sadness, despair—or just numbness. At other times there are glimpses of hope, peace, and purposefulness. The challenge is to reinvest ourselves, our relationships, the family, the job, or a surviving parent in this new world, a new world changed forever by the death of a parent. As I said earlier, healthy spirituality is always about affirmation, about believing that there is a tomorrow, an eternal expression, and reaching for it. Our reach may be tentative, arthritic with our doubts and questions, convinced that there is nothing out there. And yet making even a weak attempt takes us a long way.

Reinvestment is hard work, seldom planned, usually haphazard, but it comes as we are willing to risk the outpouring of our sorrow and the claiming or reclaiming of our memories and stories. Every loss comes with this drive to move on, although it is different for each person and for each loss. For adults dealing with the death of a parent there are tasks, issues, and feelings all blended together.

It takes time (and you should take all the time you need!):

- to want to reinvest
- to wade through that pile of bills
- to do the thank you cards, one card at a time
- to slow down (or speed up) and link anew with your spouse or partner
- to find the connection with your spiritual resources and faith
- to try again to connect with your children (they have suffered too)
- to learn the "signals" for stepping in or backing off with a surviving parent

- to clean closets; to decide about furniture, tools, pictures, "treasures"
- to eat a good meal
- to exercise
- to dare to dream
- to know and to feel that Mom/Dad is in your heart always

It is risky to suggest do's and don'ts for grievers. It becomes a checklist, someone else's "prescription," that can distract us from focusing on ourselves and our self-awareness. There are, however, a few suggestions I will make here. These are some things that have helped me in my grief work for my mother and father, some things that insight—and sometimes trial and error—has shown to be good guidelines.

Helping Yourself to Healing
1. Find safe places.

In Psalm 46, God is described as "our refuge and strength." The word "sanctuary" means a place of safe hiding, out of harm's way. Who, what, and where are your safe places? The cozy chair in the den where you do focused reading, journaling, or meditating? Your priest, minister, or rabbi, or a religious friend? The group you jog or walk with? A support group (a formal one or just a group that gathers informally over coffee with a shared commitment to each another)? Personal time for physical fitness and the letting go of troubling energies? Times of retreat and committed prayer? Safety allows us to be vulnerable; it allows us to look inward so that we can release our burdens outward.

2. *Commit to releasing.*

I have tried to emphasize that you are entitled to your feelings, that they are *your* feelings, and that it is your choice of when and how to release them. Many talk about the importance of sharing feelings. That is valuable, but some folks, at least at the start of the journey, are simply unable to share their deepest feelings with another person. To commit to "releasing" your feelings is to commit to self-respect and self-affirmation, to valuing your feelings and working with them in the way that is most healthy for you. You will know what to do as you listen to yourself while also learning from the resources, love, and wisdom that surround you.

3. *Practice healthy living.*

This is a tough one. Most of us have trouble with that even when we are not grieving. As mentioned in the first chapter, healthy choices include good nutrition. (If you need guidance, ask your physician or call your local hospital, health department, or hospice. They should be able to recommend a nutritionist or nutrition program.) Exercise is also important. Don't overdo it, but with careful and intentional exercise, you can increase your energy and decrease stress. Watch what you drink. Get plenty of rest, quality sleep (also a tough challenge for the bereaved). Finally, be intentional in maintaining and enriching your spiritual connections and resources.

4. *Pray.*

Prayer isn't about asking (well, at least not all of the time), but about relating and relationship. When the disciples marveled at Jesus' prayer life, it was because they were aware that Jesus found great strength, solace, and safety in prayer. It may also true that your prayer life was wounded in the dying of a parent. You may have prayed and prayed, yet felt that your prayers went unanswered. Find someone to talk to about this. There are "techniques" to prayer, but a skilled guide will invite you into a discussion of prayer and your relationship with God.

5. Find ways to honor and express your grief.

There are helpful resources and techniques out there that you might want to consider. Remember that what may not suit you today may be a perfect fit tomorrow. You may want to consider journaling; writing letters, articles, or other materials that tell your story; and revisiting your hobbies, especially the arts, which will help you give expression to what you are experiencing. Or you might try some of the hobbies or practices that were favorites for your parents; this could become a special bonding experience.

6. Seek counseling.

Counseling is not about being crazy (although feeling "crazy" is common to grief), but about finding a person or group where you can get information, guidance, and some structure to your journey and life experience. There are many good counselors. Make sure it is someone you feel is a comfortable fit. Also check out their comfort level with grief issues. Many therapists are unwilling to touch the depths of grief in their lives or in the lives of their clients. Your pastor or priest may be a good starting point. Contact your local hospice or the chaplain at your community hospital for recommendations.

7. Slow down.

You have all the time that you need. You may not believe that, with so many people becoming "experts" and "critics" in your life. There may be so many practical concerns, challenges, and hard work that have come with this death that you may feel rushed every moment of the day. But it is still your journey; claim the time you need, *all* the time you need.

8. Learn from your journey.

Many of you have been thrust into the systems, bureaucracies, and decisions that can leave you feeling as if you've been washed up on some very unfamiliar shores. Insurance companies, hospital bills, Social Security, cemetery requirements, veteran's benefits: the list goes on and on. You may also have wrestled with advance directives, reluctance by physicians to follow those wishes, or the inability of family members to grasp the reality of your parent's condition. Learn from this. Are there things you might want to do differently with and for a surviving parent? Are there parts of your story, your records, your advanced planning that seem inadequate or incomplete? Part of your healing is to carry on the wisdom of your parents. This is one way to do that.

Hindering Yourself When You're Hurting
1. Avoid unhealthy habits.

Poor eating habits, eating too much or too little, running from your feelings, abusive or self-destructive behavior, drinking too much of the wrong things: these habits not only hinder our reach for healing, but can bring additional problems or burdens.

2. Don't try to "go it alone" or "just be brave."

"I can handle this"; "I think I'll just dig in at work"; "If I close my eyes to this it will all go away." Moving in these directions can keep you from healing in the ways you need to heal.

3. Be alert for addictive and abusive behaviors.

Addictions and abusive or controlling behaviors (of self or others) are serious problems in society, and are never welcome in grief. The stress of dealing with the death of a parent can be particularly risky for those who have had past experiences with addictions or with abusive or destructive attitudes and behaviors. If you have had difficulties in the past, don't try to go it alone. Recognize that you may need to surround yourself with friends and sponsors who can provide a safety net at this difficult time.

*T*hought / *O*pportunity / *P*rayer

T - "It is a risk to attempt new beginnings . . . yet the greatest risk is for you to risk nothing. . . . You were strong to hold on. You will be stronger to go forward to new beginnings."

—Rabbi Earl Grollman, *Time Remembered*

O - On a sheet of paper, write down all the things you *think* you have to get done. Then prioritize them. When the list is finished pick out one "must" and one "want to." Then take a look at the list again tomorrow. It is okay to change your mind about priorities over and over again.

P - *God of all creation, Lord of time and the gift of life, help me to slow down if I must and speed up when I should. Then give me the wisdom to discern the healthy choices I must make as I strive to reinvest. Amen.*

II

Stops Along the Way

Chapter 4

Why does everyone want a piece of me?
Boundaries are important

For many of us who are grieving, we only begin to reach the real depths of our sorrow when we have moved out of the fast lane, the overdrive of caretaking, the funeral itself, and the mountain-high pile of paperwork. We have been totally immersed in tasks, decisions, and feelings. It is only as we crash or slow down that we begin to assess the impact of grief.

Life changes with the death of a parent, and that change reaches to every corner of our family. During the hard work of grieving we are often called upon to re-create our family. There are practical matters: rearranging furniture, organizing bills, making up missed appointments. We are in the pinch and press of being a family again, of becoming a new or redesigned family. So many people and tasks make claims on our time and energy.

Setting boundaries is the way we claim our territory, establish the rituals and habits that sustain us, and set apart our safe times and safe places. Part of the work of any relationship, including family relationships, is learning what our boundaries are and finding ways to communicate them—while encouraging others to do the same.

As a surviving adult child, you are reclaiming old memories and traditions, while also finding ways to express what is now unfolding. You are finding your way through territory that may be very unfamiliar. This journey requires you to work out how you will relate to a surviving parent (as discussed later), your spouse or partner, your children, your siblings, and extended family and friends. Sometimes keeping it up with it all can feel like trying to repair a bursting dike: just as you plug up one "leak," something breaks through "downstream."

I strongly suggest that you begin by committing to two absolute priorities: your own health and well-being, and the healthy remembering of your parent(s). From there, you can begin to reach out to the others. Unless you are able to first nurture your own health, interactions with others will only be draining. As you do what you need to do for yourself, you will be able to focus on others with mutual care and respect.

Here are some more specific suggestions:

1. Check in with yourself.

How are you feeling today? What do you need for yourself? What is going on in your relationships? Is it time to reach out (and possibly receive from those reaching out to you), or is it time to say, "enough"? You have no control over others, but keep in touch with yourself and keep your boundaries clear.

2. Make a list.

It may seem silly at first, but you may find it helpful to sit down with paper and pencil to make a list of the important relationships in your life. In black and white, it may be easier to see where you are spending your time now, and where you might like to spend it in the future. It may also remind you of specific issues you want to address: your spouse may be needing to re-connect with you; an important friendship may deserve some time. Taking the time to put it in writing is sometimes the first clue that these issues are there.

3. Set aside time for specific purposes.

Sometimes personal growth happens and relationships move to a deeper level just when things seem to be falling apart. Consider making "appointments" to spend time with special people, time away from distractions to discover what really matters in your relationships. It may also help to schedule time to deal with particular problems. After my father had died, one particular issue arose with my mother at a time when I was swamped at work and my sister was dealing with new health problems in her family. We simply couldn't get to it right away, but we set aside a "connection time" a few days later, which immediately lessened the frustration and tension.

4. Be open to surprises.

Surprises can come in many ways, and they do not necessarily come as problems. Someone comes forward to speak in tender ways, with special memories, of your parent or of you. You didn't plan for it, but how wonderful to welcome this bit of good news! A relative who previously seemed distant or uncaring touches you in new and dramatic ways. If we keep our boundaries and plans too rigid, we might miss these gifts. Remain open to unexpected gifts. You will find the strength to embrace them and be blessed by them.

5. Find a "safe place."

Sometimes the people closest to you, the ones you love the most, are too close to respond to your needs. When we are all consumed by the same feelings, it is difficult to give to each other the love and care we need. Yet it is at this moment that we need to sort things out, ask questions, and find clarity in the fog of grief. Seek out a person or group, or even a book, that you can turn to for refreshment and support. This kind of "time out" can enable you to step back into the family in new and healthier ways.

6. Get extra help when it is needed.

If you feel your family being torn apart, get help. If you sense your partner is more distant or that you are now distancing, get help. If you feel that positive conversation has lessened while shouting, glares, silences, or stares have taken over, get help. Maybe you just feel that some encouragement and handholding is needed. Get help. Often, our perspective is skewed by grief, and we just need someone to help us see things as they are. Even if others won't follow your lead, at least keep yourself on a healthy track. If you need someone to talk with, contact your family doctor, your local hospice, the chaplain at the hospital in your community, your clergy person, or the reference department of your local library.

Thought / Opportunity / Prayer

T - If you never say no, how will people respect your choices and decisions?

O - Make an inventory of the special people in your life. As you look through the list, focus on three things:

Thanksgiving — Give thanks that they are part of your life.

Clarification — Consider how you best can relate with each other.

Patience — Remember that they are struggling too.

P - Almighty God, I am learning so many things over again. This includes realizing where and when I can give, and whom I can lean on. It is so much work when I feel so tired. Help me focus. Let me see that I don't have to work things out without you; you will be there for me. Amen.

Chapter 5

I often feel so empty and alone.
Finding connection to spirituality

I have a story, Lord. It is about loss, but the plot
is about love. Help me to affirm and respect my
story. Guide me through it. Help me to listen to
myself in an affirming way. By the way, God—are
you listening? Amen.[1]

In my book, *HeartPeace: Healing Help for Grieving Folks,* I closed
each chapter with a prayer. The one above has facilitated consider-
able discussion in conversations and correspondence with readers,

---

[1] Gilbert, Richard, *HeartPeace: Healing Help for Grieving Folks,* p. 32.

and it is one I keep coming back to in my own journey. "Are you listening, God?"

While working on this book, I was often asked, "Is it a book on grief or a book on spirituality?" I always responded, "Yes!" You really can't do one without the other. To speak of grief, at least on a level that is genuine and honest, is to speak about spirituality. I have mentioned it throughout this book in very gentle ways, and now I want to speak directly about spirituality.

Grief is physical, emotional, and social. Most of us would not question that. We know that struggle firsthand. Grief rips into the very fiber of our being. Everything is examined, reframed, kicked about, pinched, torn, crushed, and remolded. It should be clear, then, that grief will involve our spiritual thoughts, longings, and, yes, doubts and concerns.

You may not feel particularly comfortable with religious language or even the mention of God, but that does not mean that you are not a spiritual being. Spirituality is about our most basic selves, about searching for meaning, for purpose, and, most basically, for some reason that life is worth living. It is not simply about having answers, but about the freedom and safety to explore our deepest feelings and deepest questions. Some may have very profound spiritual expressions and expectations; others may seem more comfortable with a less specific "life philosophy" or ethic. All of us, though, have questions, longings, and the challenge to reframe who we are and what we believe when we are bereaved.

When a parent dies we often experience special spiritual challenges. Christians often speak of learning the truths about God and Jesus *on the lap of our parents*. Our parents brought us to the font for baptism, "placed in our hands the holy scriptures" (as is expressed in many baptismal rites), brought (or dragged!) us to catechetical instruction and the sacraments, sat reasonably patient with us as we squirmed in the pew at worship, and tried their best to support us as we tackled our tough questions about the very existence and meaning of God.

When a parent dies it may also mean the death of our spiritual mentor, friend, and guide. The resulting feeling may be that the link, the connection to God, has died too. Grief, in this case, feels like a wilderness. The wilderness is a scriptural image for that which is devoid of familiar things. In the wilderness of a parent's death, we wrestle with life, grief, and yes, God.

There is a hopeful aspect to this experience of wilderness, though. The wilderness may also be a place where, like Jacob, we spend the night wrestling with "a stranger" only to discover, at dawn, that we are on truly sacred ground. In the struggle itself, we may find a point of connection with God.

Sometimes when we are grieving we can find religion tiresome, maybe even oppressive. At this point, traditional religious rituals only remind us that Mom or Dad has died rather than offer us comfort. We enter church and see a casket rather than the symbols we long for. We grow weary of fellow church members who often seem insensitive to our plight or offer those meaningless or hurtful remarks. We wonder why our clergy person seems distanced or won't stop by for a visit.

If you are feeling overwhelmed, step aside from some of the customs and people, but don't step aside from your pain. Stay with the questions, wounds, and despair. Stay with the doubts. Stay with the questions, "Why did Dad have to die now?" "Why did she have cancer?" "Why did the treatments fail?" and the many other questions that come from your heart. These are ultimately questions about God. You may never get "the answers" that will make everything right, but the questions are the pathways where you will meet God and, ultimately, yourself.

> Again, from *HeartPeace*:
>> It is such a bumpy ride, Lord. Detours. Potholes. New questions. More losses. With every acknowledgment of loss the pain rises to the top. Will I ever heal, Lord? Stay with me, God ... please?! Amen.[2]

Of course, others may find the very opposite of what I have mentioned here. Your faith and your community of faith may have been sources of great comfort during your grief. Even in the midst of loss, this a gift worth celebrating.

[2] Gilbert, p. 32.

Thought / Opportunity / Prayer

T - "O Lord, thou knowest how busy I must be this day: if I forget thee, do not thou forget me."
 —Sir Jacob Astley

O - Look at your calendar or appointment book. Can you write in an "appointment" with God? If it works once, try it again—and again.

P - *Dear Jesus, you invited us to come to you and to place our burdens on you. Help me to believe that you really mean it. Amen.*

III

Traveling With a Surviving Parent

Chapter 6

I still have *one parent.*
Surviving with a surviving parent

One of my fondest memories of the church picnics I attended as a child was the annual tug-of-war contest. After much groaning and effort, someone won, someone lost, we all ended up in the mud, and then we celebrated with ice cream.

Tug-of-war is a wonderful game, but when we try to pick up with day-to-day life after the death of a parent, you may find yourself involved in a version of tug-of-war that you don't enjoy at all. In a time when you want and need to support each other, you may find that you and your surviving parent seem to be pulling against one another. You may feel that you are giving every bit of effort you have, and yet more is demanded.

There are so many specific issues that can come up when dealing with a surviving parent, but there is one principle to keep in mind, no matter what you are facing at the moment: communicate. It is crucial that you communicate with your surviving parent. That, of course, is easier said than done. What does communicating entail? Let me offer a little more thorough explanation. There are a number of actions that are called for here:

- remember
- realize
- respect
- ritualize
- resources
- reach
- rest

Remember

Good communication includes remembering that *all* of you are grieving. You are learning the reality and struggle of being a grieving adult child. Your surviving parent is faced with a different realization: *I am a widow/widower.* You have your own experiences and needs. It is important that you get time, space, and some respect. Offer the same to your parent.

Realize

Realize that death does not necessarily change long-established patterns of relating. It is terribly frustrating for many, but parents often continue to treat adult children as children, pushing them aside when parent and child most need to lean on each other. I remember a family in which a father died. The surviving spouse was devastated and feeling so alone. I offered to call her children (fifty-two and fifty-eight years old), and was asked not to. "I must be strong for the sake of the children," she said. It is important for adult children simply to be aware of these dynamics. Don't crush them too quickly; they may be the only familiar ground for your parent. On the other hand, there comes a point when you must challenge these old patterns of relating and open up the possibility of something new.

Respect

Respect your surviving parent's feelings, decisions, and attitudes. Sometimes families rush in to clear the closets (and the memories) and make many decisions about the house, schedules, living arrangements, and finances. My mother lost a great deal when my father died. I felt that it was important that we not take even more from her by excluding her from decisions, demoting her to the level of a child. Don't get ahead of where your parent is and needs to be.

Ritualize

Your mom or dad lived a life full of rituals, just as we all do. Who sits in which chair at breakfast and reads which section of the newspaper first. Who cleans. Who cuts the grass. Who remembers to put the garbage out on Wednesday. Who sleeps on which side of the bed. These are rituals, ways we learn to do things together and to give meaning to who we are and what we share. The death of a loved one is often felt most sharply when it comes to these very routine habits or rituals. To have these small rituals overturned can be devastating.

To "ritualize" means to invite your surviving parent—along with other members of the family—to claim new meaning through new rituals or restored rituals. At the same time, these new rituals also become ways to remember the deceased. When I went home to cut the grass or deal with the storm windows in the porch for Mom, I was stepping in for Dad and reminding myself and the rest of my family of him. Other rituals you might take up include:

- a trip to the gravesite combined with a meal eaten out.
- new (perhaps more elaborate) ways to celebrate your parent's birthday.
- a simple lunch date as a way of remembering the birthday of the parent who has died.
- vacationing with your surviving parent. (Is there somewhere both of you long to go?)
- going to the movies (or a ball game) together on a certain day each month.
- including your surviving parent in your own family's big events and rituals.
- establishing a special spot (indoor or out) as a memorial to the parent who has died.

Resources

Keep track of the significant resources in your surviving parent's life: the doctor, attorney, banker, financial consultant, lawn service, accountant. Let them know who you are and how you can be reached, and make them aware of ways they can assist your mother or father. Also remember other resources, including Medicare, health insurance supplements, Social Security, IRS, etc. Your surviving parent may be apprehensive when it comes to these individuals or organizations. A parent who has never completed a tax form may become very upset as April 15 approaches.

Learn who and what is of concern to your parent and how to work with those providers and your parent.

Reach

Extend your love and time as overtures of care for your surviving parent. They are trying to find their own way, and the loneliness can be devastating. Keep reaching out. Your parent may say "no" a lot, but this may also be a way of saying, "I am so glad you asked; I just need more time." Keep reaching out. Also be alert for the times when Mom or Dad is reaching out to you.

You can also reach out on behalf of your mother or father to those around them. Many surviving parents feel they have lost access to their social world. If a husband always drove, his wife may have no way to go shopping or to church programs. If husband and wife were partners in card games, a widower may now feel excluded from an evening of cards. Friends and colleagues may feel awkward around a grieving friend and back away, consciously or unconsciously. Unfortunately, this only creates additional losses when survivors desperately need a friend. You may have to put in a word of encouragement to a friend or neighbor. You would be amazed how therapeutic it is when someone stops by for a cup of coffee or to discuss last night's ballgame.

Finally, you may have to reach out in encouraging your parent to connect spiritually. Grief is a profoundly spiritual experience, as we discussed in the last chapter. Sometimes the practical matters of life, including time, and transportation, can vastly affect our relationship with God or our religious community. For some, the death of a loved one creates deep questions or a sense of betrayal by God. Consider ways you can encourage or enable your parent in his or her spiritual life.

Rest

Sometimes we have to call a "time out," putting our feelings, grief issues, or some very practical problems on hold. Sometimes that need for rest also means taking "time off" from Mom or Dad, especially if he or she is very demanding or very clingy. Of course your parent has very valid needs, but they should not be met at the expense of your own well-being or the health of your marriage and family. Keep your boundaries clear, and don't feel that you have to spend *all* of your waking moments with Mom or Dad.

Thought / Opportunity / Prayer

T - "As I search for my loved one, I will hold the harsh realities at bay. I miss them and love them. When I am ready, I can look within my own heart and life, for they are with me always."
——Elizabeth Levang and Sherokee Ilse,
Remembering with Love

O - Gather together a large envelope and several 3" x 5" cards. On each card, write the words "I remember…" and describe something special that you remember about the parent who has died or an event or occasion at which you can clearly picture him or her. Consider sharing these cards with your surviving parent. It may be an easy way to spark a healing conversation, in which you can share your memories with one another.

P - *God of all of my thoughts and feelings, you are affirming and supportive. I know that you care about me and about my parent who is now alone. Give us both courage and wisdom. Help us to recognize our sadness and also to celebrate our happy memories. Teach us both how to move into the future. Amen.*

Chapter 7

Someone is taking over for the parent I've lost.

Additions, not replacements

Few aspects of the grief following a parent's death prompt more discussion, anxiety, and discomfort than a new love interest for the surviving parent. Last year I offered more than half a dozen seminars on surviving the holidays while grieving. At every one of them, those who had lost a parent lined up, wanting to talk about (and sometimes complain about!) such a relationship in their family.

This is not always an issue that is addressed with adults who have lost a parent; some consider it an issue only if one is a *child* when the parent dies. Listening carefully, though, has revealed to me that the emotional issues for adults are very real. They may speak of their concern for the surviving parent ("Mom is too distressed to concentrate on another relationship"), but underneath, rooted deeply in their own feelings and grief issues, is the fear that this new relationship may take the surviving parent away from them or erase the memory of the parent who died. It can be a powerful emotional reaction, prompted by what feels like a new loss. Those of us in this situation fear that a new "mom" or "dad" will *replace* the parent who has died.

This sense of loss can lead to a disruption of family harmony as we lash out at the surviving parent for "forgetting" or "dishonoring" the parent who died. This is an area in which it is often especially difficult for us to understand the needs or feelings of our surviving parent, and, indeed, the intensity of our own feelings can surprise us. Family communication (along with family healing) runs the risk of grinding to a halt.

Of course, the first step is to become aware of the losses and fears that are involved for us as we watch a parent in a new relationship. As we address these fears directly, we will find it easier to see this "new love" as an *additional* love, not a *replacement*. Working through the issue together can actually bring new love and peace to a family where everyone shares the common sorrow of a parent/spouse who has died. As always, this is easier said than done. Let me here suggest three aspects of this experience that are especially important as you find your own way: First, where is your parent in all of this? Second, where are you (and the family) in all of this? Finally, how can you listen and learn together for the good of all concerned?

Mom or Dad is entitled to his or her own journey, and sometimes that journey includes various levels of community, friendship, and intimacy. Many times a surviving parent has been on a much longer grief journey, beginning with the very first visit to the surgeon for a biopsy, while his or her children are "catching up." A widowed spouse also experiences loss on a tremendous variety of levels: he or she is stripped of routine, rituals, support, a best friend, maybe financial assistance and transportation, and, yes, intimacy. Your parent may conceal this from you, but he or she most likely is experiencing deep feelings of loneliness. There are days that tears are shed, feelings are poured out, friends call or stop by, but the one thing that would feel good would be a hug. Many surviving parents have lived in relationships that were so dependent or interdependent that loneliness itself becomes a death sentence, and a relationship seems the only spark of life and meaning for them.

On the other hand, entering into a new relationship may not be easy. Many men have particular difficulties with new relationships. Some recent studies have suggested that men struggle because the waves of intimacy around feelings leave them confused (and unskilled). In the end, the question of whether your parent is ready for a new relationship must be his or her own decision, made with the support and encouragement of family.

Track your own issues, needs, and feelings as these issues come up. Simply put, is your "protest" about your surviving parent and this new relationship or is it related to your grief over the parent who died? Pay attention to your grief issues, but remember that they are your issues, not your surviving parent's. Seek the wise counsel of trained professionals or selected friends who can empathize with your expressions without "taking sides." As you interact with your surviving parent, avoid criticism, judgment, or ultimatums.

Remember, you have already "lost" a parent and do not need any more losses.

Find ways to journey together with others, and that may include welcoming a new person into your story. Be open to sharing rituals, telling stories, and, yes, remembering in healthy ways the parent who has died. The new person in your mother's or father's life will welcome those stories and memories, as long as he or she is welcomed as an individual and not forced to compete with your deceased parent.

*T*hought / *O*pportunity / *P*rayer

T - "There are things that are known and things that are unknown: in between are doors."
—— Elizabeth Levang and Sherokee Ilse,
Remembering with Love

O - Using boxes (charting), circles, sketches, or symbols, draw a picture of your family. As you name each member of the family you will want to include your deceased parent. Isn't there room for an additional name?

P - *There is so much here, God, that I do not understand and I may not like. You are the source of love, patience, insight, courage, and hope. Help me to mirror your gifts and, as I am able, to embrace new members of the family. Amen.*

Chapter 8

I never expected this.
Aging: new challenges with a surviving parent

Just after my father died, there were many occasions of insight, reassurance, and awareness that were a big help for my mother. Even though there were some very tough moments, we shared, remembered, told stories, and even had some fun outings.

Then it all changed. Things slowed down. Mom was more forgetful. She began to have mental lapses that the doctors attributed to "something medical," although the tests never revealed what. All that the rest of us knew was that something had changed. It was getting harder to cope.

You may not have been pulled into the dilemma of medical problems or other challenges, but sooner or later, most of us have another great hurdle ahead: the approaching death of a second parent. As a friend remarked in her recent Christmas letter, "Dad had died long ago, and we knew, with Mom's health problems, that she was soon to die. In the care of hospice she died in peace and surrounded by the reassurances of her faith ... *but nothing prepared me for this.*"

The death of a surviving parent is the final reminder that neither Mom nor Dad will be here for us, that we are now the elders of the family, and that, on some level, we are now on our own. Saying goodbye was tough once, and we wanted it to be a one-time thing. On some level, we never believed that a second round of goodbyes would be ahead for us.

Your surviving parent's movement toward death may be quiet and peaceful. On the other hand, you may have been called on to make dramatic changes in your family, living arrangements, financial plans, and how you use your time. You may be experiencing his or her growing dependence upon you. The parent now with you—because of strokes, dementia, or Alzheimer's—may not be the person you have known and loved for years. You suddenly feel called upon to welcome a "stranger" while at the same time saying goodbye to the parent you love.

And there are other challenges that may come your way. There can be the challenge of closing down a house filled with memories and memorabilia as you consider a nursing home or other placement options for Mom or Dad. I remember having to close down an eleven-room house, with fifty-three years of memories, in two days. It was so unfair. The pressures of the calendar robbed us of remembering dinnerware and furnishings, pictures and height measurements by the kitchen door, outdoor parties and sneaking a kiss with that first boyfriend or girlfriend. Others may be called upon to assume major financial burdens for nursing home or other bills, coming to harsh awareness that our parent's financial resources just will not cover all of the expenses. In order to care for a parent, you may be making tough choices that carry many costs, including emotional ones.

In so many ways, this final goodbye is painful.

In the bibliography are listed some excellent resources that can be starting points for you as you explore where you are on your journey and tend to the work that now awaits you. The challenge is to capture and cherish the good stories of Mom and Dad, while at the same time doing the work you must do and tending to your own needs and those of your family.

Think back to the reminders that were given earlier. Don't forget your well-deserved "time-out" moments. Respect your needs and feelings, and, as you are able, the needs of those who surround you. Focus on making good, healthy choices. Even now, work to keep your boundaries clear.

I still remember the roller coaster ride that my father and mother both experienced in their desire to live life while also facing their own dying. It all seemed so unfair. We had to battle medical personnel who handled some things insensitively and who, at times, seemed to dismiss our urgency, questions, and apprehensions. At one point, my family came to the difficult point of feeling that it would be best to let my father end his life peacefully, and yet doctors wanted to pump in more and more medicine, perform more and more tests. Then, after his death, we watched my mother in profound sadness, wondering whether there could be any life for her after my father's death.

And yet, during the same period, there were also wonderful moments. Stories shared. Laughter roared out over the clouds of sadness. Tears lessened and we witnessed a hint of a smile. So it can be for all of us. Recollections step in where voids used to dominate. There is death, but there is life that lives beyond death, eternally, for our parent(s), and for us as we continue our journey of living and cherishing.

*T*hought / *O*pportunity / *P*rayer

T - "In the midst of sickness [aging, dying] your loved one [parent] is helping you to confront life, finding comfort in your crisis, and acceptance in your anguish."
—Rabbi Earl Grollman,
Caring and Coping When Your Loved One Is Seriously Ill

O - Take a time out. Choose something that sounds good just for *you*. As you are able, invite in your family, maybe even your surviving parent.

P - *Suffering? More sadness? Battling with Medicare and bureaucrats? Why, God, why? Are you there? I need you to walk with me now. Amen.*

IV

Solitary Paths

Chapter 9

My tears were shed long ago;
why are they here again?
Childhood losses experienced all over again

You may find yourself drawn to this book, not because your parent's death was recent, but because you still sense the ways in which it affects your life.

We should begin with some facts about children and grief, facts which, sadly, are often not recognized:

- Children grieve.
- Children often grieve alone.
- Children can carry early losses into their adult life!

- You never fully "get over" the death of a parent, especially when it occurs in childhood.
- After many, many years, there can still be parts of your story left to talk about.
- Even though your parent died long ago, there is still time to talk about your losses, remember things from childhood that may need some tender care, and grieve now for a parent from long ago.

This chapter will be very brief. Please think of it as an invitation to take a look at your own story if you are one of the many adults who have grieved a parent since childhood. Bringing the issue up now doesn't mean that you didn't grieve as a child, or that the adults in your life weren't sensitive and caring. It does mean that you always will miss your parent and that, as you continue on in life—perhaps becoming a parent yourself—you will discover in new ways what you may have "missed" because your parent died so long ago.

Some of this book may be helpful to you; some of it may not. Please receive it as an opportunity to claim your grief story and experience it in new and supported ways.

*T*hought / *O*pportunity / *P*rayer

T - No one can say when your grieving is "finished." If now is the time to remember a loss from long ago, receive this opportunity as a gift and use it in healing ways.

O - "I remember…" Take time to remember the years gone by and the losses you have experienced. You may have lost not only a relationship with a parent, but many other little things along the way. This may be the time also to say, "I remember," for those parts of your story.

P - *O God, you are timeless, as is your love and care. You are never too busy to listen to the stories and feelings of long ago. As you affirm them, you affirm me. Encourage me to find new ways to share. Amen.*

Chapter 10

I have some very deep wounds.
Even those can be healed

Relief is a common part of grief. When my father died, my family experienced a measure of relief. Dad's suffering was over and, for us, the suffering of a particular chapter in this journey had ended. We could have a funeral liturgy rich in celebration, with brass, percussion, and great singing, a glimpse of the hope and "relief" that are the gifts of the risen Christ.

For some adults, the death of a parent brings a different kind of relief. It is the relief that the adult child's *own* suffering is over. It is a glimpse of hope, peace, and safety, maybe, for the first time, because a parent has died. This is the relief felt by those who ask,

- Why should I grieve a parent who abused my Mom (or Dad) constantly for years?
- Why should I grieve a parent who was always drunk, who robbed me of my childhood innocence, and forced me to miss out on the best times of my life?
- Why should I grieve a parent who beat me (and my siblings) over and over again?
- Why should I grieve a parent who sexually violated me?
- Why should I grieve a parent who was never there for me?

When I give talks on grief, I offer words intended to comfort. Often, I suggest, "The love that is now lost is the love that will sustain you and lead you to life and healing." For most of us, this is very true. For some, though, this means nothing and serves only to heighten the rage and discount the wounds that are very real and very deep. For those who have experienced pain at their parents' hands, the grief to be dealt with is much more complicated than simply grieving one person's death. This grief is about many, many deaths:

- The death of safety
- The death of love
- The death of innocence
- The death of family
- The death of childhood
- The death of peace
- The death of self-esteem
- The death of a sense of purpose
- The death of parent/child roles and rules

The sword of abuse rips deep into the victim and it wounds many relationships, roles, and expectations. The sword crushes how we feel about life, family, self, even the God who is supposed to be a loving shepherd who protects us from these horrors. These scars are deep and deadly, and the long-term effects are real. The cycle of abuse realized as a child becomes normative, the yardstick by which we measure and experience everything that follows in life. Hard work is required in order to choose alternate styles of life, in order to nurture the ability to love oneself and reach out to new expressions of love with others.

There are no shortcuts, no easy ways out, when you are experiencing grief of this kind. First, you must allow yourself to feel the desperate need to protest the injustice. Often, it seems safer to continue a long-established habit of hiding feelings, rather than to risk showing the depths of your pain and losing the one safe place you have. But expressing those feelings is the beginning of a path of healing.

Here are just a few suggestions as you continue to move along that path, summed up by a few key words:

- Respect
- Recognize
- Reach
- Receive

Respect

Respect yourself, your feelings (including the scars), and all of your story. You have run, lashed out, and buried deep, and although those strategies may have "worked" for you for a time, they aren't working now. Don't be afraid to say that what happened to you was *wrong*. Respect all that you have lost because of the mistakes of another person. All of those need to be grieved. Respect the fact that these feelings are buried deep and that you deserve care and support.

Respect the fact that others have been hurt as a result of your hurts. They will need to find their own way and may not always "be there" with you and for you. Respect them even when they cannot understand what you are going through. Respect the pathway to healing. You cannot undo what has happened, and you cannot repair or fix what has been or what should have been. What is past is past. Today and tomorrow are up for grabs and it is your grip that matters.

Recognize

Recognize what is happening. Recognize that your inner world is a "construction zone," and slow down in the work zone. Recognize when family and friends are reaching out to you, even in their own pain, to be present with you. Recognize when you need to reach out to others and take that risk.

Recognize that you may have to reach beyond yourself and the familiar surroundings of your story to get the help you need. Therapy, counseling, medical care, spiritual direction: these are gifts that can move you along on your journey to freedom from the scars that control you.

Reach

Reach for the things you desire most deeply: meaningful relationships, a happy family, happy and safe children, good job performance, good health, the ability to sleep through the night without nightmares or other disruptions, financial security, friends, the right and opportunity to be playful, to enjoy life, to have fun.

Reach for the resources that can help you, as mentioned above. If you do not know where to start, or are embarrassed to ask, seek a safe starting point. Check your telephone directory for mental health or counseling centers. The public library has information. The funeral director, who may have known many of the "secrets" anyway, will know the people who can help. Call your local hospice or the chaplain or social worker at your hospital. Ask your family doctor. Understand that your story will not always come easily. Some resources may not "fit" at first, and yet will be very helpful later.

Remember the spiritual connections discussed in Chapter 5. Explore your spiritual resources. Pray. Read scripture. Explore the religious rituals that once were important to you or that now appeal to you. Reach into your feelings so that you can reach to others who await you and need you: a surviving parent (most likely also a victim), your spouse and children, your siblings who have spent a lifetime burying the secrets (just like you!). Reach out to the networks that bring together programs and friends who really do understand, at least part of your story. A.A., Al-Anon, A.C.O.A., bereavement support groups: there *are* people who understand.

Receive

Receive at least the *possibility* of relief, of healing. Receive the help of people who love you and have loved you through all of this. Be open to the resources that professionals can bring you. Recognize that love and care come in strange places, in unexpected voices, memories, gestures, and words, and welcome them. Receive the help of your religious community, of prayer offered for you from others, of the presence of God in worship, in the sacraments, or in the symbols or practices of your tradition.

Most of all, be open to receiving *yourself*. You may find that you will become able to appreciate and delight in yourself in ways you never imagined.

*T*hought / *O*pportunity / *P*rayer

T - "We are as broken puzzle pieces, tapestries with twisted threads. Yet, puzzles can be re-assembled to form different pictures. Tapestries can be mended by weaving new threads into place. . . ."

—Darcie Sims, *Footsteps Through the Valley*

O - "I remember. . . ." "I want to forget. . . ." "I want life to be. . . ." You have hard work ahead of you but, sometimes in unexpected ways, healing will come.

P - *Forgiveness. Peace. Life. Hope. Reconciliation. I always thought those were your words, God. There was no room for them in my life or in my family. Could they become my words, too? Amen.*

Chapter 11

I've experienced a "double whammy."
Adopted—when you feel a little different

I have a remarkable sister. Becky and I grew closer (despite a difference in ages that meant more as children) during my father's suffering and dying and my mother's sorrow, suffering, and death. We were there for each other, we found special ways to bring out the strengths in each other, and we found memories, stories, hugs, and words that brought the desperately needed comfort in our own journey.

My sister understood that, when Dad and Mom died, it was particularly tough for me. I experienced a "double whammy." I have lost *four* parents, two who gave me away, and two who took me in. I was adopted. In the third grade my parents explained this fact to me, as if revealing a deeply guarded family secret. The words fell like a bomb. In many ways life for me stopped in the third grade, and even decades later, in counseling, this issue created explosions of emotion that caused additional challenges and crisis for me.

As I was able to let the rays of light of hope and love in, very gentle reassurances from family, my wonderful wife, and my dear daughter, I could begin to accept this part of my story. It hasn't been easy, for them or for me, for the feelings of abandonment that can accompany adoption are very strong "filters."

There is a growing awareness of what it means to be adopted. Jewel Among Jewels is a national support organization, with a very fine newsletter, for adults dealing with their own adoption and for adopting parents. Today, there is improvement in how adoptions are handled and how adoption is perceived. On the other hand, there is still much work to be done for the adopted and in awakening the general public.

For me, the scars of adoption led me to feel, "I am different; someone didn't want me; I was a bad boy," and, ultimately, "I am all alone." When first my father and then my mother died, I not only experienced the deep losses associated with each of those relationships, but I also lost any hope of knowing my full history, my story. In a profound and deeply painful way, I was all alone.

Counseling became very important. My sister was wonderful. Uncle and cousin drew closer, even though they probably knew nothing of these "secret" scars. My wife and daughter were and are wonderfully supportive. With their help, I began to express and face my own feeling that, "I am the little boy that nobody wanted."

In this realm, as in others, the healing comes slowly, but it does come. Facing this issue is a challenge, but it is also the only pathway to wholeness. As I allow the scars to be as much a part of my story as anything else, amazingly, they begin to shrink. That becomes the only true hope for those of us who have experienced this "double whammy."

*T*hought / *O*pportunity / *P*rayer

T - "He destined us for adoption as his children through Jesus Christ."
—Ephesians 1:5a

O - What scars do you have? When do you find that they cause you the most pain? Are you willing to share these scars with a skilled listener or a cherished friend?

P - *O God, over and over you speak of a love between us that can never be interrupted or blocked. It becomes easy to question this when my scars run deep. You respect my scars, but love me more. Help me to give all of this over to you. Amen.*

V

A Final Word

Dear friend,

Thank you for letting me step into your story and walk awhile with you on your journey. I count it a privilege, and it has also been a gift to me in my own healing. To share with you from my story has enabled me to share something of my mom and dad, and that is a giant step toward healing and peace for me.

Our parents greeted us at birth. They were there for our first steps, our first friends, schools, cars, dates, and, for many of us, a new family. They were always "there," with us in a very special way. In some part of ourselves, we expected them to live forever. But now they have died, thrusting us into this wild ride we call grief. We have joined the ranks of many people like us who have had to come to terms with life without one or both parents.

It is my hope that something in this book touched you in a special way. Maybe it was some information about grief, approval of some of your tougher feelings, some clarity on a very foggy day. Maybe you captured a moment of sanity and safety as you explored the wounds, unfinished business, or hurts that have stayed with you.

Throughout this book, I have offered simple insights through brief quotations, through suggested tasks and exercises, and through invitations to spiritual expression. These resources are intended to transform this book from words to read to pathways to follow. May that be its gift to you. You deserve the best.

Richard Gilbert

VI

Resources

A. Scripture, hymns, and prayers

Scripture

From the Psalms

Psalm 23. The Lord is my shepherd, I shall not want. He makes me lie down in green pastures; he leads me beside still waters; he restores my soul. He leads me in right paths for his name's sake. Even though I walk through the darkest valley, I fear no evil; for you are with me; your rod and your staff they comfort me. You prepare a table before me in the presence of my enemies; you anoint my head with oil, my cup overflows. Surely goodness and mercy shall follow me all the days of my life, and I shall dwell in the house of the Lord my whole life long.

Psalm 27:1, 13-14. The Lord is my light and my salvation; whom shall I fear? The Lord is the stronghold of my life; of whom shall I be afraid? I believe that I shall see the goodness of the Lord in the land of the living. Wait for the Lord; be strong, and let your heart take courage; wait for the Lord!

Psalm 34:8. O taste and see that the Lord is good; happy are those who take refuge in him.

Psalm 46:1-2. God is our refuge and strength, a very present help in trouble. Therefore we will not fear, though the earth should change, though the mountains shake in the heart of the sea.

Psalm 121. I lift up my eyes to the hills—from where will my help come? My help comes from the Lord, who made heaven and earth. He will not let your foot be moved; he who keeps you will not slumber. He who keeps Israel will neither slumber nor sleep. The Lord is your keeper; the Lord is your shade at your right hand. The sun shall not strike you by day, nor the moon by night. The Lord will keep you from all evil; he will keep your life. The Lord will keep your going out and your coming in from this time on and forevermore.

From the prophet Isaiah

Isaiah 25:6-9. On this mountain the Lord of hosts will make for all peoples a feast of rich food, a feast of well-aged wines, of rich food filled with marrow, of well-aged wines strained and clear. And he will destroy on this mountain the shroud that is cast over all peoples, the sheet that is spread over all nations; he will swallow up death forever. Then the Lord God will wipe away the tears from all faces, and the disgrace of his people he will take away from all the earth, for the Lord has spoken. It will be said on that day, Lo, this is our God; we have waited for him, so that he might save us. This is the Lord for whom we have waited; let us be glad and rejoice in his salvation.

Isaiah 40:1-8. Comfort, O comfort my people, says your God. Speak tenderly to Jerusalem, and cry to her that she has served her term, that her penalty is paid, that she has received from the Lord's hand double for all her sins. A voice cries out: "In the wilderness prepare the way of the Lord, make straight in the desert a highway for our God. Every valley shall be lifted up, and every mountain and hill be made low; the uneven ground shall become level, and the rough places a plain. Then the glory of the Lord shall be revealed, and all people shall see it together, for the mouth of the Lord has spoken." A voice says, "Cry out!" And I said, "What shall I cry?" All people are grass, their constancy is like the flower of the field. The grass withers, the flower fades, when the breath of the Lord blows upon it; surely the people are grass. The grass withers, the flower fades, but the word of our God will stand forever.

From the New Testament

John 10:11-16. "I am the good shepherd. The good shepherd lays down his life for the sheep. The hired hand, who is not the shepherd and does not own the sheep, sees the wolf coming and leaves the sheep and runs away—and the wolf snatches them and scatters them. The hired hand runs away because a hired hand does not care for the sheep. I am the good shepherd. I know my own and my own know me, just as the Father knows me and I know the Father. And I lay down my life for the sheep. I have other sheep that do not belong to this fold. I must bring them also, and they will listen to my voice. So there will be one flock, one shepherd."

John 14:1-6. "Do not let your hearts be troubled. Believe in God, believe also in me. In my Father's house there are many dwelling places. If it were not so, would I have told you that I go to prepare a place for you? And if I go and prepare a place for you, I will come again and will take you to myself, so that where I am, there you may be also. And you know the way to the place where I am going." Thomas said to him, "Lord, we do not know where you are going. How can we know the way?" Jesus said to him, "I am the way, and the truth, and the life. No one comes to the Father except through me."

1 John 3:1-2. See what love the Father has given us, that we should be called children of God; and that is what we are. The reason the world does not know us is that it did not know him. Beloved, we are God's children now; what we will be has not yet been revealed. What we do know is this: when he is revealed, we will be like him, for we will see him as he is.

Hymns

"Jerusalem, the Golden"

Jerusalem the golden, with milk and honey blest,
beneath thy contemplation sink heart and voice oppressed;
I know not, oh, I know not, what joys await us there;
what radiancy of glory, what bliss beyond compare!

—**Bernard of Cluny**

"Abide With Me"

Abide with me: fast falls the eventide; the darkness deepens;
Lord, with me abide: when other helpers fail and comforts flee,
help of the helpless, O abide with me.
I fear no foe, with thee at hand to bless; ills have no weight,
and tears no bitterness. Where is death's sting? Where, grave,
thy victory? I triumph still, if thou abide with me.

—**Henry Francis Lyte**

"Rock of Ages"

Rock of ages, cleft for me, let me hide myself in thee;
let the water and the blood from thy wounded side that flowed,
be of sin the double cure, cleanse me from my guilt and power.

—**Augustus Montague Toplady**

"O For a Closer Walk With God"

O for a closer walk with God, a calm and heavenly frame,
a light to shine upon the road that leads me to the Lamb.
So shall my walk be close with God, calm and serene my frame;
so purer light shall mark the road that leads me to the Lamb.

—William Cowper

"My Faith Looks Up to Thee"

While life's dark maze I tread, and griefs around me spread,
be thou my guide; bid darkness turn to day; wipe sorrow's
tears away, nor let me ever stray from thee aside.

—Ray Palmer

Prayers

In remembrance

O God, thank you for the life of my parent(s), _____, whom I remember as I read this book and reflect on my journey. You have welcomed my loved one to the light of your eternal glory. As we travel through this darkness we call sorrow, brighten my heart and my feelings with the light of your love. Amen.

As you grieve

Hear me, O God. The days often seem so long, so empty. It isn't because I lack things to do. I just miss Mom/Dad so much, and everything seems so different. This grief is real, and it's messy, God. Bring order to my life and comfort to my family. You are my sensibility. Amen.

It has been a good day, O God. Thank you for a measure of peace and hope so I could get through all the things I had to do. Amen.

As you grieve with your family

Caring God, you speak powerfully of the gift of family. A death has disrupted the family we have known and loved. My mom/dad is now bearing a new label, "widow/widower." I can't understand that journey or those feelings, only my own. Help us to support one another and respect each other's unique needs and hurts, and equip us so we can bear something of your love to and for each other. Amen.

Lord of the Holy Family, and God of our family, we have been touched by death, and also have lived through the time of dying.

We need to get reacquainted in many ways, to look at rituals lost and rituals redefined, and just to find time for each other. Help us to be sensitive to one another, patient and forgiving. Be our guide and strength. Amen.

I haven't been as helpful to my family as I should be. It just seems more than I want to tackle these days. Yet they keep understanding, loving me. Thank you for my family. Help me to spend more time with them. Amen.

Some rough spots came today, God. What makes it worse is that I just don't know why. What set all this off? Now we are shouting instead of listening, and the anger level is mounting. Help us to respect the pain and to work through it, but step in so that the pain doesn't overwhelm us. Amen.

Your Son, O God, invited children to come to him. We are all children of God. Keep us mindful of the grief needs of children. They do grieve. Sometimes we are so close to them that we cannot always see their struggles. At other times we appear distant, safely removed so that they do not know of our willingness to help. We are a family, and that includes the children. May we be there for each other. Amen.

Give me patience, God. I know the children miss Grandpa/Grandma. It's just that they have so many questions, and I am running out of answers. Could it be more about sharing and less about answers? Show me the way. Amen.

B. Printed and recorded resources

Books

1. General grief

While most of these resources do not specifically address the grief issues of adult children, they have much to offer you. They also can help put much of what you are experiencing into a helpful perspective as you move into the larger family of the bereaved. Sometimes resources are hard to find. If you need any help please feel free to contact The World Pastoral Care Center by phone at 219/464-8183 or by e-mail at <rgilbert@valpo.edu>.

Resources marked with a * are of particular value for those grieving a violent death.

Alexander, Paul. *Wrap Myself in a Rainbow: A Grief Guide and Healing Workbook*. New York: Crossroad, 1995.

Davies, Phyllis. *Grief: Climb Toward Understanding*. San Luis Obispo, CA: Sunnybank Publishers, 1998.

Del Zoppo, Patrick. *Mourning*. Staten Island, NY: Alba House, 1995.

Fitzgerald, Helen. *The Mourning Handbook*. New York: Simon & Schuster, 1994.

Gilbert, Richard. *Responding to Grief: A Complete Resource Guide*. Point Richmond, CA: Spirit of Health!, 1997.

Grollman, Earl. *Living When a Loved One Has Died*. Boston: Beacon Press, 1995.

*Henry-Jenkins, Wanda. *Just Us*. Omaha: Centering Corporation, 1998.

Hope for Bereaved. Syracuse: Hope for Bereaved, 1995.

Levang, Elizabeth and Sherokee Ilse. *Remembering with Love: Messages of Hope for the First Year of Grieving and Beyond*. Minneapolis: Deaconess Press, 1992.

Manning, Doug. *Don't Take My Grief Away: What to Do When You Lose Someone Close.* San Francisco: Harper & Row, 1979.

McNees, Pat. *Dying: A Book of Comfort; Healing Words on Loss and Grief.* Garden City: Doubleday, 1996.

Meyer, Charles. *Surviving Death: A Practical Guide to Caring for the Dying and Bereaved.* Mystic, CT: Twenty-Third Publications, 1997.

Miller, James E. *Welcoming Change: Discovering Hope in Life's Transitions.* Minneapolis: Augsburg, 1997.

Miller, James E. *What Will Help Me? 12 Things to Remember When You Have Suffered a Loss.* Fort Wayne: Willowgreen, 1994.

Miller, James E. *Winter Grief, Summer Grace: Returning to Life After a Loved One Dies.* Minneapolis: Augsburg, 1995.

Pfeiffer, Joseph Robert. *A Different Season: A Practical Guide While Grieving a Death.* Memphis: Landscapes Publishing, 1997.

Ryan, Karlene Kay. *To Find Hope: Simple Wisdom for Those Who Grieve.* New York: Paulist Press, 1997.

Sims, Darcie. *If I Could Just See Hope.* Wenatchee, WA: Big A & Co., 1996.

Sims, Darcie. *TouchStones: On Your Journey Towards Hope.* Wenatchee, WA: Big A & Co., 1993.

Smith, Harold Ivan. *Death and Grief: Healing through Group Support.* Minneapolis: Augsburg, 1995.

Staudacher, Carol. *A Time to Grieve: Meditations for Healing After the Death of a Loved One.* San Francisco: Harper, 1994.

2. For adults grieving the loss of a parent

Akner, Lois F. *How to Survive the Loss of a Parent: A Guide for Adults.* New York: Quill, 1993.

Curry, Cathleen. *When Your Parent Dies.* Notre Dame, IN: Ave Maria Press, 1993.

*Davis, Jeffrey M. *The Shadow of Evil: Where Is God in a Violent World?* Dubuque, IA: Kendall-Hunt Publishing, 1996.

Donnelly, Katherine Fair. *Recovering from the Loss of a Parent.* New York: Berkley Books, 1993.

Myers, Edward. *When Parents Die: A Guide for Adults.* New York: Penguin Books, 1986.

Smith, Harold Ivan. *On Grieving the Death of a Father.* Minneapolis: Fortress, 1994.

3. For surviving spouses

Campbell, Scott and Phyllis Silverman. *Widower: When Men Are Left Alone.* Amityville, NY: Baywood Publishing, 1996.

Curry, Cathleen. *When Your Spouse Dies.* Notre Dame, IN: Ave Maria Press, 1990.

Felber, Marta. *Grief Expressed: When A Mate Dies.* West Forks, AR: Life Words, 1997.

Floyd, Maita. *Platitudes: You Are Not Me.* Phoenix: Eskualdun, 1991.

Heinlein, Susan, et al. *When a Lifemate Dies: Stories of Love, Loss & Healing.* Minneapolis: Fairview Press, 1997.

Lambin, Helen. *The Death of a Husband: Reflections for a Grieving Wife.* Chicago: ACTA, 1998.

Miller, James E. *Autumn Wisdom: Finding Meaning in Life's Later Years.* Minneapolis: Augsburg, 1995.

Vogt, Robert L. *The Death of a Wife: Reflections for a Grieving Husband.* Chicago: ACTA, 1996.

4. On spiritual aspects of grief

Gilbert, Richard B. *HeartPeace: Healing Help for Grieving Folks.* St. Meinrad, IN: Abbey Press, 1996.

Guntzelman, Lou. *So Heart and Mind Can Fill: Reflections for Living.* Winona, MN: St. Mary's Press, 1998.

Howard, Evan Drake. *Suffering Loss, Seeking Healing: Prayers for Pain-Filled Times.* Mystic, CT: Twenty-Third Publications, 1996.

Mundy, Linus. *What Helps the Most ... When Hope Is Hard to Find.* St. Meinrad, IN: Abbey Press, 1996.

Mundy, Linus. *What Helps the Most ... When You Lose Someone Close.* St. Meinrad, IN: Abbey Press, 1996.

O'Brien, Mauryeen. *Praying Through Grief: Healing Prayer Services for Those Who Mourn.* Notre Dame, IN: Ave Maria Press, 1998.

5. When surviving parents are struggling

Albom, Mitch. *Tuesdays with Morrie.* New York: Doubleday, 1998.

Byock, Ira. *Dying Well: The Prospect for Growth at the End of Life.* New York: Riverhead, 1997.

Grollman, Earl. *Caring and Coping When Your Loved One Is Seriously Ill.* Boston: Beacon Press, 1995.

Grollman, Earl. *When Someone You Love Has Alzheimer's.* Boston: Beacon Press, 1997.

Hayslip, Bert, Jr. *Helping Older Adults Cope with Loss.* Dallas: TLC Group, 1995.

Meyer, Charles. *A Good Death: Challenges, Choices and Care Options.* Mystic, CT: Twenty-Third Publications, 1998.

Miller, James E. *One You Love Is Dying: 12 Thoughts to Guide You On the Journey.* Fort Wayne: Willowgreen, 1997.

Miller, James E. *The Caregiver's Book: Caring for Another; Caring for Yourself.* Minneapolis: Augsburg Publishing, 1996.

Morgan, John D., ed. *Ethical Issues in the Care of the Dying and Bereaved Aged.* Amityville, NY: Baywood Publishing, 1996.

Oliver, Samuel. *What the Dying Teach Us: Lessons on Living.* Binghamton, NY: Haworth Press, 1998.

6. For men

Golden, Thomas R. *Swallowed by a Snake: The Gift of the Masculine Side of Healing.* Kensington, MD: Golden Healing Publishing, 1996.

Golden, Thomas R. and James E. Miller. *When a Man Faces Grief; 12 Practical Ideas to Help You Heal from Loss.* Fort Wayne, IN: Willowgreen Publishing, 1998.

Miller, Robert J. *GriefQuest: Reflections for Men Coping with Loss.* Winona, MN: St, Mary's Press, 1999.

7. For women

Clayton, Jean. *Women in Mourning.* Omaha: Centering Corporation, 1996.

Dotterweich, Kass P. *Grieving as a Woman: Moving Through Life's Many Losses.* St. Meinrad, IN: Abbey Press, 1998.

8. For young children

Flynn, Jessie. *Holidays and Special Days.* Louisville: Accord, 1994.

Flynn, Jessie. *Hospice Hugs.* Louisville: Accord, 1996.

Flynn, Jessie. *A Little Talk with God.* Louisville: Accord, 1994.

Flynn, Jessie. *What Happens When Someone Dies.* Louisville: Accord, 1994.

Hodge, John. *Finding Grandpa Everywhere: A Young Child Discovers Memories of a Grandparent.* Omaha: Centering Corporation, 1998.

Jordan, Mary Kate. *The Weather Kids: Sometimes Sad Things Just Happen.* Omaha: Centering Corporation, 1993.

Liss-Levinson, Nechama. *When a Grandparent Dies.* Woodstock, VT: Jewish Lights, 1996.

Morning, Barbara. *Grandfather's Shirt.* Omaha: Centering Corporation, 1994.

Richmond, Judy. *Just You and Me.* St. Joseph, MO: Hands of Hope Hospice, 1998.

Scrivani, Mark. *Love, Mark II.* Syracuse: Hope For Bereaved, 1990.

Stillwell, Elaine. *Sweet Memories: For Children and Adults . . . To Create Healing and Loving Memories for Holidays and Other Special Days.* Omaha: Centering Corporation, 1998.

9. For teens and young adults

Grollman, Earl. *Straight Talk About Death for Teenagers.* Boston: Beacon Press, 1994.

O'Toole, Donna. *Facing Change: Falling Apart and Coming Together Again in the Teen Years.* Burnsville, NC: Compassion Books, 1995.

Scrivani, Mark. *Griefjourney.* Syracuse: Hope For Bereaved, 1996.

10. For holidays and special days

Alexander, Paul. *A Ray of Hope: Facing the Holidays Following A Loss.* Rockville Centre, NY: Paul Alexander Productions, 1995. (video)

Flynn, Jessie. *Holidays and Special Days.* Louisville: Accord, 1994. (for children)

Ilse, Sherokee. *Coping with Holidays and Special Days.* St. Paul, MN: A Place to Remember, 1994.

Lowery, Missy. *Not Just Another Day: Families, Grief and Special Days.* Omaha: Centering Corporation, 1992.

Miller, James E. *Helping the Bereaved Celebrate the Holidays.* Fort Wayne, IN: Willowgreen Productions, 1998.

Sims, Darcie and Sherry Williams. *Holiday Help: A Guide for Hope and Healing.* Louisville: Accord, 1996.

Journals/Magazines

There are many newsletters and journals available for the bereaved and those who provide comfort and care. The one journal that consistently addresses grief on a first-person level, covering a wide range of issues and feelings, is *Bereavement Magazine*. For information, call 888/604-HOPE.

Recorded resources

Paul Alexander offers a wide range of recorded resources, including many of his own compositions, in both compact disc and cassette format. For information or to receive a catalog, call 800/538-4158.

About Tomorrow is a collection of thoughts, dialog, and music edited by Fred Frank. It offers insight, direction, information, and comfort. For information contact Comfort Music, P.O. Box 3403, San Clemente, CA 92674. By e-mail, <comfortmus@aol.com>.

C. *Organizations and support programs*

AARP provides an excellent program, *Widowed Persons Service*, along with many helpful publications. For information contact Susan Kovac Eckrich, manager, AARP Grief and Loss Programs, AARP, 601 E. Street, NW, Washington, DC 20049. 202/434-2277. You can also visit their web site at www.aarp.org/griefandloss.

The National Catholic Ministry to the Bereaved offers membership services, a resource library, retreats and programs, networking, and support. 606 Middle, Elyria, OH 44035. 440/323-6262.

Abbey Press offers an extensive listing of brochures (*CareNotes* and *Teen Notes*) and very affordable books for adults and children. Over 100 titles. For information, or to request a catalog, call 800/325-2511.

ACCORD Aftercare offers a variety of programs and support services geared especially to the funeral industry. They have many brochures and other printed resources that would be especially helpful for general reading. For information and a listing of available resources call 800/346-3987.

If you are in need of counseling assistance and are not sure who to call, contact your local hospice or ask an area chaplain. To contact a chaplain, call The Association of Professional Chaplains at 847/240-1014. To contact a local hospice, check your telephone book or public library or contact The National Hospice Organization, 1901 N. Moore, Suite 901, Arlington, VA 22209. 703/243-5900.

If you have other needs, contact The World Pastoral Care Center by phone at 219/464-8183 or by e-mail at <rgilbert@valpo.edu>.